Author's No

This book features 100 influential and inspiring quotes by Rumi. It's amazing that his wisdom still resonates in today's life. Hopefully it will be a great source of inspiration for you!

1

"Laugh as much as you breathe.
Love as long as you live."

2

"In your light I learn how to love. In your beauty, how to make poems. You dance inside my chest where no-one sees you, but sometimes I do, and that sight becomes this art."

3

"Let your teacher be love itself."

4

"Whenever we manage to love without expectations, calculations, negotiations, we are indeed in heaven."

5

"On the path of love we are neither masters nor the owners of our lives. We are only a brush in the hand of the master painter."

6

"Love is the bridge between you and everything."

7

"This is love: to fly toward a secret sky, to cause a hundred veils to fall each moment. First to let go of life. Finally, to take a step without feet."

8

"Love risks everything and asks for nothing."

9

"Wherever you are, and whatever you do, be in love."

10

"Every moment is made glorious
by the light of love."

11

"Love sometimes wants to do us a great favor: hold us upside down and shake all the nonsense out."

12

"A thousand half-loves must be forsaken to take one whole heart home."

13

"Let yourself be drawn by the stronger pull of that which you truly love."

14

"Let the lover be disgraceful, crazy, absentminded. Someone sober will worry about things going badly. Let the lover be. "

15

"Reason is powerless in the expression of Love."

16

"Love is not an emotion, it's your very existence."

17

"Close your eyes, fall in love,
stay there."

18

"When I am with you, we stay up all night.
When you're not here, I can't go to sleep.
Praise God for those two insomnias!
And the difference between them."

19

"Every story is us."

20

"Is it really so that the one I love
is everywhere?"

21

"I am yours. Don't give myself
back to me."

22

"Lovers find secret places inside this violent world where they make transactions with beauty."

23

"I once had a thousand desires.
But in my one desire to know
you all else melted away."

24

"There are lovers content with longing. I'm not one of them."

25

"Gamble everything for love, if you're a true human being."

26

"If you want to be more alive,
love is the truest health."

27

"We are born of love; Love is our mother."

28

"Love calls – everywhere and always.
We're sky bound.
Are you coming?"

29

"You were born with wings, why prefer to crawl through life?"

30

"Life is a balance of holding on and letting go."

31

"Before death takes away what you are given, give away what there is to give."

32

"The woman has great power. She can tie knots in your chest that only God's breathing loosens. Don't take her appeal lightly."

33

"Out beyond ideas of wrongdoing and rightdoing, there is a field. I'll meet you there. When the soul lies down in that grass, the world is too full to talk about."

34

"With life as short as a half taken breath, don't plant anything but love."

35

"If you want money more than
anything,
you will be bought and sold.
If you have a greed for food,
you will become a loaf of bread.
This is a subtle truth.
Whatever you love, you are."

36

"I am not this hair, I am not this skin, I am the soul that lives within."

37

"People who repress desires often turn, suddenly, into hypocrites."

38

"Beauty surrounds us, but usually we need to be walking in a garden to know it."

39

"You think you are alive
because you breathe air?
Shame on you,
that you are alive in such a
limited way.
Don't be without Love,
so you won't feel dead.
Die in Love
and stay alive forever."

40

"It's your road, and yours alone.
others may walk it with you,
but no one can walk it for you."

41

"Live life as if everything is rigged in your favor."

42

"You think of yourself as a citizen of the universe. You think you belong to this world of dust and matter. Out of this dust you have created a personal image, and have forgotten about the essence of your true origin."

43

"You know the value of every article of merchandise, but if you don't know the value of your own soul, it's all foolishness."

44

"The world is a mountain, in which your words are echoed back to you."

45

"Travelers, it is late.
Life's sun is going to set.
During these brief days that you
have strength,
be quick and spare no effort of
your wings."

46

"There is a candle in your heart,
ready to be kindled.
There is a void in your soul,
ready to be filled.
You feel it, don't you?"

47

"Where there is ruin, there is hope for a treasure."

48

"When you go through a hard period, when everything seems to oppose you, when you feel you cannot even bear one more minute, never give up! Because it is the time and place that the course will divert!"

49

"I have lived on the lip
of insanity, wanting to know
reasons,
knocking on a door. It opens.
I've been knocking from the
inside."

50

"If you desire healing,
let yourself fall ill
let yourself fall ill."

51

"Put your thoughts to sleep, do not let them cast a shadow over the moon of your heart. Let go of thinking."

52

"Give up to grace. The ocean takes care of each wave 'til it gets to shore. You need more help than you know."

53

"Do not feel lonely, the entire universe is inside you. Stop acting so small. You are the universe in ecstatic motion. Set your life on fire. Seek those who fan your flames."

54

"Wherever you stand, be the soul of that place."

55

"Your light is more magnificent than sunrise or sunset."

56

"Shine like the whole universe
is yours."

57

"Only from the heart can you touch the sky."

58

"Who could be so lucky? Who comes to a lake for water and sees the reflection of moon."

59

"As you start to walk on the way, the way appears."

60

"Be motivated like the falcon,
hunt gloriously.
Be magnificent as the leopard,
fight to win.
Spend less time with
nightingales and peacocks.
One is all talk, the other only
color."

61

"People want you to be happy. Don't keep serving them your pain. If you could untie your wings and free your soul of jealousy, you and everyone around you would fly up like doves."

62

"Gratitude is the wine for the soul. Go on. Get drunk."

63

"Be empty of worrying.
Think of who created thought!"

64

"Why do you stay in prison
When the door is so wide open?"

65

"Don't make yourself miserable with what is to come or not to come."

66

"Respond to every call that excites your spirit."

67

"Why should I be unhappy? Every parcel of my being is in full bloom."

68

"On a day
when the wind is perfect,
the sail just needs to open
and the world is full of beauty.
Today is such a day."

69

"When you do things from your soul, you feel a river moving in you, a joy."

70

"But listen to me. For one
moment
quit being sad. Hear blessings
dropping their blossoms
around you."

71

"Knock, And He'll open the door
Vanish, And He'll make you
shine like the sun
Fall, And He'll raise you to the
heavens
Become nothing, And He'll turn
you into everything."

72

"Be a lamp, or a lifeboat, or a ladder. Help someone's soul heal. Walk out of your house like a shepherd."

73

"Very little grows on jagged rock. Be ground. Be crumbled, so wildflowers will come up where you are."

74

"If you want to win hearts, sow the seeds of Love. If you want heaven, stop scattering thorns on the road."

75

"Be kind and honest, and harmful poisons will turn sweet inside you."

76

"My dear heart, never think you are better than others. Listen to their sorrows with compassion. If you want peace, don't harbor bad thoughts, do not gossip and don't teach what you do not know."

77

"Yesterday I was clever, so I wanted to change the world. Today I am wise, so I am changing myself."

78

"Don't be satisfied with stories,
how things have gone with
others. Unfold your own myth."

79

"Your heart is the size of an ocean. Go find yourself in its hidden depths."

80

"Let yourself be silently drawn by the strange pull of what you really love. It will not lead you astray."

81

"Moonlight floods the whole sky from horizon to horizon; How much it can fill your room depends on its windows."

82

"Within tears, find hidden laughter."

83

"Seek treasures amid ruins, sincere one. Seek treasures amid ruins, sincere one."

84

"There is a secret medicine given only to those who hurt so hard they can't hope. The hopers would feel slighted if they knew."

85

"All people on the planet are children, except for a very few. No one is grown up except those free of desire."

86

"Your task is not to seek for love, but merely to seek and find all the barriers within yourself that you have built against it."

87

"Do you pay regular visits to yourself? Start now."

88

"Your heart and my heart are very, very old friends."

89

"If you are looking for a friend who is faultless, you will be friendless."

90

"I love this world, even as I hear the great wind of leaving it rising, for there is a grainy taste I prefer to every idea of heaven: human friendship."

91

"Be with those who help your being."

92

"I love my friends
neither with my heart nor with
my mind.
Just in case...
Heart might stop.
Mind can forget.
I love them with my soul.
Soul never stops or forgets."

93

"Friend, our closeness is this: anywhere you put your foot, feel me in the firmness under you."

94

"Words are a pretext. It is the inner bond that draws one person to another, not words."

95

"My heart, sit only with those who know and understand you."

96

"Goodbyes are only for those
who love with their eyes.
Because for those who love with
heart and soul there is no such
thing as separation."

97

"Don't grieve. Anything you lose comes round in another form."

98

"Moonlight floods the whole sky from horizon to horizon; How much it can fill your room depends on its windows."

99

"Be full of sorrow, that you may become hill of joy; weep, that you may break into laughter."

100

"Very little grows on jagged rock. Be ground. Be crumbled, so wildflowers will come up where you are."